Self-Esteem

Powerful Neuro-Linguistic Programming Techniques To Drastically Enhance Your Self-Esteem For A Successful Life

(Self-Belief Is Crucial For Achieving Personal Success)

Noble Warner

TABLE OF CONTENT

What Precisely Is Low Self-Esteem? 1

Confront Your Fears 16

Quit Burging Around Little Mistakes. 28

    How to Become More Self-Assured 32

Resources To Fight Your Fears 39

Self-Compassion Is Essential For Long-Term Self-Esteem 50

Self-Esteem And Self-Confidence: What Are They? 87

A Guide For Developing Characteristics Of High Self-Esteem 100

Realistic Steps To Teach Mindfulness: 108

What Precisely Is Low Self-Esteem?

The idea of low self-esteem is straightforward: it is the belief that one is inadequate, incapable, and incompetent. When persistently negative self-beliefs create an unconscious behaviour pattern that feeds back those ideas in the person's head, these concepts could set off a dangerous cycle. They say to themselves, "You can see that my actions show how inadequate I am. I, therefore, have the right to believe that I am unqualified and inept." The mental pattern endures, and the beliefs get stronger over time.

When you don't think well of yourself, you typically display the following symptoms:

You make an effort to complete things accurately.

You feel unworthy of love and are afraid to love others. You assign blame to others for your mistakes and shortfalls.

You constantly see the bad side of everything. You prefer to be cautious and are reluctant to take risks, even small ones.

You have a very low regard for everyone, including your loved ones.

You might rather delegate decision-making, especially important ones, to others.

You have to understand that low self-esteem is a learned behaviour. That suggests that your low self-worth emotions were either instilled in you by another person or developed as a result of your overstretching of a few negative events.

This is great news since it can change learned behaviour by forming new beliefs. An authoritative figure, parent, or caregiver can negatively impact a person's self-belief. A child or teenager who looks up to that person feels as though they have let him down in some way.

This results in the behaviours we just covered, which are indicative of low self-esteem. Overgeneralization and generalization happen when you try to generalize the conclusions of a particular scenario to your entire life. A man with low self-esteem may feel that no woman would be interested in him if he asks a woman out and she says no. A man who has high self-esteem is more likely to understand that a woman's "No" only means that she isn't interested in him.

The result of low self-worth

Life is affected in many aspects by low self-esteem. You need to have some confidence in your ability to succeed if you want to improve your life and take fearless steps toward your goals. "Whether you feel you can or you cannot, you are right," Henry Ford once said. Ford's remark holds today just as it did back then. It is only through progress that you may venture into the unknown.

You can never be sure you will succeed when you venture into the unknown. On the other hand, you can have faith in your ability to learn, overcome challenges, and go past whatever barriers you may come across. How much you believe in yourself is determined by your level of self-esteem. When your self-esteem is high, you will believe in yourself without wavering, and you will be more resilient when faced with challenges. When you have low self-esteem, you'll be more likely to buckle under pressure and worry excessively about your abilities.

What consequences may low self-esteem have? Your level of self-belief has a huge impact on your overall health and is often closely correlated with it. Those who have a low opinion of themselves usually suffer from the following effects:

Easily demoralized

They suffer from hair and skin issues.

Fearful and uneasy

continually wind up in shaky, perhaps fatal, partnerships

extremely protective

Addiction to drugs and alcohol

experience eating problems

inadequate immune and cardiovascular systems

Heart issues are exacerbated by worry and stress.

Promiscuous behaviour involving multiple partners

However, why should you give a damn?

Let's consider how someone with poor self-esteem goes about managing life. When faced with hardship, such individual typically "locks up" because negativity consumes their thoughts. That individual will think poorly of themselves. Although they will feel helpless, they will actually feel as though the world is crumbling around them. Feelings of being stuck or undeserving are caused by low self-esteem, among many other factors that I shall discuss later.

Now, though, we ought to consider people who have a strong sense of self-worth and how they handle hardship. High self-esteem leads to better coping mechanisms. Even though failures and losses are unpleasant, people who have a high sense of self-worth usually move past their negative emotions. Adversity might be seen as a teaching opportunity by this person because they believe they are capable and deserving. Rather than criticizing themselves for a circumstance, they are making every effort to resolve the issue.

Our sense of self also influences our social behaviour. Pro-social behaviour, or just being kind and empathic with others, is exhibited by those who have a high sense of self-worth. This promotes the healthy growth and upkeep of wholesome interpersonal relationships, which in turn fosters the creation of even more fulfilling life experiences. Furthermore, having a high sense of self-worth helps you see things clearly and manage stress better—a valuable skill at some of the most trying times in your life.

All of the information you've read, plus the knowledge that your general well-being would increase, make improving your self-esteem seem like an important reasons to take action. Even so, you might not be persuaded enough to give it much mind, so let's explore what occurs if your poor self-esteem persists.

Concerns Regarding Low Self-Esteem

Even when you don't want it, poor self-esteem is unavoidable. There are times in life that will knock you down a few pegs, just as I discovered both as a teenager and when raising my teenagers. You will occasionally have situations that will pull you in the other direction, and having a very high feeling of self-worth is indeed attainable.

You will be able to move across it as your life changes, much like a spectrum might. But the times that really affect you are the ones that appear to last the longest, and they might affect you in a lot of different ways.

It Influences Your Response to Life.

As previously said, having a strong sense of self-worth enables one to overcome some of life's most difficult obstacles. You are able to let go of the negative and begin moving in the direction of something better. When you're lugging around poor self-esteem, the reverse occurs. You get more wise to those disappointments and the criticism that follows them. If your self-esteem is low, you may even start reacting negatively to other people's issues.

It's challenging to control your feelings when you react more strongly to life. It's as if you've lost your healthy outlook on life and are unable to function or think like a reasonable human being. This may also cause you to exaggerate the importance of relatively little problems.

It turns into the "Bad Day" That Never Gets Better.

Since that's typically what happens when someone descends that scale to low self-esteem, it might be assumed that they are having a horrible day. You spend the rest of the day feeling depressed after failing a test or getting into a fight with one of your parents. You react more strongly to events in your day, but you get over it by the next day.

When you struggle with self-worth, a terrible day never goes away. You perceive everything in your life as negative, regardless of how good or neutral it may be. You get isolated from others as a result, and you find yourself stuck in a pattern that you find difficult to change.

It Could Easily Develop Into Depression.

I used to be one of the many people who thought that depression was the root cause of low self-esteem. But it's actually the exact opposite. This vicious loop of negative self-talk that low self-esteem produces can lead to a whole new set of difficulties, including depression, anxiety, and a host of other difficult-to-treat mental health conditions.

I would want to talk about this for a bit. Even though this book is meant to support you through difficult times, books cannot solve all mental health problems. It is best to seek assistance if you apply any of the strategies in this book and experience no change.

You give yourself the ability to take major steps toward your goals by incorporating the Three Cs of goal-setting into your strategy. Your choices and actions are guided by clarity, which gives you a distinct sense of direction. Your motivation, tenacity, and resilience are fueled by commitment, which helps you overcome obstacles. By being consistent, you can stay on course, make steady progress, and avoid the traps of inconsistency and procrastination.

It's critical to keep in mind that the Three Cs are related and supportive of one another rather than being stand-alone ideas. Your commitment is strengthened by clarity since it is simpler to remain committed when you know exactly what you are aiming for. Your commitment fuels your consistency since it keeps you focused and motivated to take consistent action. As each little step forward increases confidence and strengthens your sense that your goals are achievable, consistency, in turn, reinforces your clarity and commitment.

Clarity, a strong commitment, and consistency are the building blocks that help you build a framework that helps you achieve your goals.

THE THREE RS IN SETTING GOALS

A framework for creating objectives that are significant, reachable, and rewarding is provided by the Three Rs of goal-setting: realistic, relevant, and rewarding. To fully grasp the importance of each of these concepts in the goal-setting process, let's take a closer look at each one.

Practical

If you want to position yourself for success, you must set realistic goals. By establishing realistic goals, you make sure that they are doable and reachable, given your existing situation, capabilities, and resources. It entails taking into account the realistic elements of your objectives, such as the time, energy, and expertise needed to achieve them. Realistic objectives create reasonable expectations for you and take into consideration any limits or limitations you may have. You can prevent yourself from being frustrated or disappointed by setting reasonable goals. Instead, because you are aware that you can achieve the objectives you have set for yourself, you build a foundation of self-assurance and drive. This boosts your confidence in your capacity to accomplish them, which enhances the likelihood that you will remain dedicated and driven throughout the process.

Applicable

Another crucial component of goal-setting is relevance. Relevant goals are in line with your long-term aims, values, and interests. They hold significance for you and aid in your development on a personal or professional level. When your objectives are meaningful, they connect with your innermost hopes and dreams, providing you with a feeling of direction and purpose. This alignment of your values and ambitions fuels your drive and dedication. Goals that are relevant to you help you stay focused and involved since they reflect your values. They give you a direct line of sight from your actions to your overarching life vision. You may make sure that your efforts are focused on what makes you happy and fulfilled by choosing goals that are meaningful to you.

gratifying

The satisfying part of goal-setting acknowledges the advantages and rewards that come with reaching your objectives. You can increase your desire and dedication to pursuing your goals by recognizing and appreciating the benefits that come with reaching them. Intrinsic rewards include feelings of fulfilment, achievement, and increased self-assurance. They may also be external, like material gains or acknowledgement. The prizes function as indicators of advancement and a constant reminder of the importance and influence of your work. When you see the benefits of reaching your objectives, they give you a sense of drive and fulfilment.

Confront Your Fears

You must confront your worries if you want them to go away! You should be motivated to take on your fears if you truly want to broaden your horizons. When you take a chance and do something you're frightened of, a couple of things can happen. You first begin to comprehend the false beliefs that people hold about various cultures, faiths, and geographical regions. Second, you broaden your horizons and discover that you are capable of achieving even the most terrifying goals. Third, as a result of your singular experiences, you begin to think differently and broaden your possibilities.

How, then, do you deal with your fears? These are the various actions you can take to transform your fears into your passions.

I. Recognize that all share fears. Without feeling guilty or harsh with yourself, admit the things you are scared of.

II. Jot down your concerns. Do you understand why these things frighten you? When you conquer a fear that you listed here, make sure you check it off and write down your revised strategy on a different sheet of paper.

III. Are a few of your worries well-founded? Some things are legitimately terrifying! It is not necessary to update the extremely harmful items that you have listed on your list. What about your unfounded anxieties, though? After you've determined which of your anxieties are illogical and which are sensible, you may begin to modify your perspective on them.

IV. Overcome your illogical fears. Proceed cautiously and divide your unreasonable anxieties into manageable activities. For example, avoid going to the top of the Eiffel Tower first thing if you are afraid of heights!

After completing every small action on your list, consider conquering your larger anxieties like skydiving, riding a Ferris wheel, or taking a hot-air balloon ride! You may discover your passion.

V. Appreciate the present. As you work through your worries, focus on the here and now and try not to worry about the future. Bring yourself to the present now, relax your body, and pay attention to your breathing.

VI. Take stock of your prior achievements. Yes, you have probably done something even scarier or something that has helped you overcome your fear. Just recalled how incredible it felt to overcome your prior fear in order to push yourself even more right now.

It's time to set your life goals once you've travelled to new places and, through self-belief and conquering your fears, found new passions.

Trying to find out why I wasn't given the same in return.

It is only natural for someone who has experienced unrequited love to want explanations. The psychological process of looking for answers and comprehending why love was not returned will be examined in this fourth chapter. Although this search might be difficult and emotionally taxing, it is a necessary step toward emotional development and self-awareness.

The need to make sense of the unexplainable

When someone feels unloved, they could feel compelled to look for explanations for why things are the way they are. This inquiry is an attempt to make sense of the unexplainable and give the emotionally trying event some meaning. It might be quite difficult to comprehend why the other person does not love you back, but this is a normal aspect of grieving and coming to terms with loss.

The inward self-examination: What went wrong?

Asking oneself what could have gone wrong is a typical tendency in the quest for solutions. The person might examine her behaviour and speech for hints that could clarify why there was no love correspondence. This procedure can cause him to feel insecure and guilty, believing that his mistakes caused an undesirable outcome.

The Need for Approval: Do I Deserve Love?

Unrequited love has the power to undermine one's self-worth and self-esteem. Searching for evidence that you are lovable and worthy of reciprocation can also be part of the quest for solutions. This need for approval may be an attempt to soothe insecurities and self-doubt.

The fear of being abandoned and rejected

Deep-seated feelings of abandonment and rejection can surface when looking for answers. The person can worry that he will never have a deep connection with another person or that his lack of love is a sign of low self-esteem. It can be tough to open yourself up emotionally in future relationships because of these crippling worries.

Idealization's function: placing the cherished person on a pedestal

An additional factor that may surface in the quest for solutions is the idealization of the cherished one. The person can elevate the other person on an emotional pedestal by emphasizing their good traits and downplaying their flaws. Because the loved one is viewed as almost flawless, this idealization might exacerbate the unease caused by the mismatch.

How to evaluate unclear signals

Uncertain signals or cordial gestures could be interpreted by the person searching for answers as a potential love interest on the other person's behalf. These readings have the potential to prolong emotional suffering and foster false hope. It's critical to develop the ability to discern between the ambiguous and obvious signals of love correspondence.

The significance of embracing uncertainty

Many times, conclusive answers are not found in the hunt for them. For a variety of uncontrollable factors, the other person might not have returned the love. In these circumstances, it's critical to develop an attitude of acceptance for the unknown and acknowledge that there won't always be a reasoned, coherent explanation for loss.

The process of accepting and grieving

Finding solutions is a crucial step in the mourning and acceptance process. It is normal for the person to want to know what went wrong and why it happened in that particular way. It's crucial to understand, though, that this procedure can take some time and that answers might not come right away or satisfy you completely.

Self- reflection's function in emotional development

Seeking solutions can also present a chance for introspection and emotional development. Through this process, the person might learn more about her relationship requirements and wants, as well as recognize behaviour patterns that may have contributed to the problem.

Constructing an inspiring story of triumph

The person can construct a story of personal development and progress as he moves through the grieving and search phases. He can choose to concentrate on how this experience has changed him and the priceless lessons he has learnt along the way rather than just dwelling on the reasons why he was not returned.

In summary, the importance of finding solutions during the healing process

Finding solutions is a normal and essential step in the grieving process for love that was not returned. It makes sense that the person is looking for affirmation and significance in the circumstance, as well as wanting to know why it was not returned. It's crucial to understand, though, that finding the solutions might be challenging and that accepting and mending can take time.

In order to achieve emotional development and healing on this road, self-reflection, accepting uncertainty, and creating an overcoming story are essential components. It is crucial to keep in mind that, despite the suffering, there remain chances for personal development and novel emotional experiences down the road. Unrequited love does not determine a person's value or worth. The person can progress toward a more emotionally rich and fulfilling existence with time, the right kind of emotional support, and self-care.

.5 The Road to ADHD Expertise

Most children diagnosed with ADHD continue to have symptoms well into adulthood. A lifetime diagnosis of adult ADHD is linked to lower levels of education and occupation, lower income, a higher incidence of comorbid psychiatric problems, and, predictably, lower levels of hopefulness and self-acceptance than for people without ADHD, regardless of whether these symptoms persist as a full syndrome or in residual form.

While medication is the mainstay of treatment for adults with ADHD, more than half of these individuals require additional support. Although psychotherapists treating adult ADHD have few guidelines at their disposal, many persons with the disease still require further psychosocial therapy due to persistent symptoms or major functional issues like procrastination, poor problem-solving skills, and disorganization.

ADD By Using a Cognitive-Behavioral Method

Both the client's notebook and the therapist's handbook are included in the treatment plan. This is the adult ADHD psychosocial treatment manual with scientific foundations. It should be regarded as a significant and long-overdue addition to the clinical literature on ADHD just for that reason alone.

This treatment plan is the same one that was applied in a randomized controlled trial study to 31 people who still had symptoms of ADHD. The majority of people with ADHD have experienced several things that have made them feel like failures, frustrated, and like they haven't lived up to their potential.

These encounters frequently leave a person with a persistently negative view of life and themselves. Cognitive behavioural treatment (CBT) offers a framework for recognizing and changing the excessively gloomy thought patterns of individuals with ADHD.

By using this approach, people can develop the resilience needed to keep using their coping mechanisms in the long run.

The remaining two days of the course cover the fourth and final module, "Additional Skills," which addresses procrastination concerns and relapse prevention. Relapse prevention is a key component of CBT and is required for the successful treatment of ADHD.

Quit Burging Around Little Mistakes.

Permit yourself to make errors. It is ridiculous to strive for perfection in everything. Give up being so hard on yourself when you make a few small errors. It's not feasible for anyone to excel at everything they do despite everyone's desire to do so. Instead, concentrate on enhancing your advantages. Never give up if you've made a lot of mistakes in your life—that's how we learn.

However, since it makes it possible for you to feel compassion for yourself, stopping self-criticism is essential to raising your self-esteem. Self-criticism typically involves talking badly to yourself and focusing on your shortcomings, which can eventually lead to a pessimistic mindset and low self-esteem. Giving up on your self-criticism enables you to grow in kindness and self-compassion.

You don't have to blame yourself for your alleged shortcomings; instead, you can take a more reasonable and practical approach. Acknowledge that making errors is a necessary and normal part of learning and developing. If you want to strengthen your feeling of self-worth, you must accept who you are and be proud of your skills and achievements.

Rather than criticizing your own perceived flaws, you might take a more pragmatic and well-rounded approach. Acknowledge that making errors is a normal and essential component of learning and development. You may cultivate a more positive self-image and boost your self-esteem by changing your perspective to one that is more focused on self-improvement than self-judgment. Healthy self-esteem growth requires accepting who you are and appreciating your accomplishments and qualities.

Being gentle and understanding with oneself is essential to boosting self-esteem. One method to achieve this is to break the pattern of criticizing even the smallest of errors.

Acknowledge that no one is flawless and that aiming for perfection is unattainable and draining. Accept imperfections. Accept your flaws as distinctive features that define who you are.

Concentrate on your successes and Celebrate and give thanks for all of your achievements, no matter how small. Instead of concentrating on your flaws or weaknesses, turn your attention to your accomplishments and the things you are pleased with.

Try not to set yourself up for disappointment by having reasonable expectations for yourself. Think about what you can actually accomplish, given your situation and skill set. You may steer clear of needless disappointment and self-criticism by setting reasonable goals.

Give up clinging to your life.

Some people complain about everything in life, including their neighbourhoods, families, unsatisfactory friends, and a host of other issues. "What you can achieve without complaining is pity from others," says the saying. I don't think it's something you want, but remember that others will think you're a loser if they sympathize with you.

Having a sense of entitlement or not being grateful for what you have are common causes of complaints. Once you quit whining, you'll have more time to express gratitude for all of your blessings. You'll feel happier and more content overall if you do this. Your self-esteem will increase as you put more optimism and thankfulness into your life.

You may take charge of your life and feel more empowered if you stop moaning. You may get victimized into believing that you have no power over your pleasure when you complain.

However, if you quit whining, you'll be able to see that you are in charge of altering your situation and improving your life.

Overall, you can cultivate a more optimistic outlook, improve your problem-solving abilities, encourage thankfulness and self-empowerment, and advance your personal development if you quit whining about your circumstances. You can develop a more confident sense of self and increase your self-esteem by doing all of these activities.

How to Become More Self-Assured

When I said that you should cultivate your inner confidence, you might have thought I was kidding, but I wasn't. You will never be able to be satisfied with a woman until you are happy with yourself. You'll always be questioning your abilities, her affection for you, and your masculinity in terms of maintaining her interest. Do you really want that? I'm assuming you purchased the book in an attempt to transform yourself, gain more self-assurance, and feel better about the version of yourself that you show the world. Let's explore what it takes to cultivate the inner self-assurance you require to feel comfortable approaching her.

● Are you one-legged only?

● Do you own flaws that you are powerless to correct?

● Do you have poor or sluggish habits?

A woman finds a man with one leg to be equally as attractive as one with two. She is not going to stare at the legs. This is what I say for a purpose. We are given what we are as individuals in life. Being a self-assured single man and being a one-legged man with a complex are two very different things. Women will notice the difference, so how do you think you'll be attractive to them if you find yourself repulsed by who you are? You have to deal with a variety of imperfections, including:

● The ones you have control over ● The ones you cannot

You must decide which is which in order to acquire confidence. You must also conclude that the only way you can ever become confident is to accept the things you cannot change. But there are things you can alter, and that's possibly where your issues are. How can you expect her to regard you as anything other than a fumbling idiot if you have a complex about the way you present yourself to the other sex? She just accepts what YOU put in front of her; YOU present yourself.

You have likely encountered overconfident men who have no justification. These people are egoists who display their fearlessness to the outside world, but they do it in a way that brings undue attention to themselves. That's not the goal you have in mind. Women are highly discerning individuals who are quick to spot pretence. You shouldn't imagine that acting rudely will make her like you. It won't. There's a significant distinction between having confidence and projecting excessive confidence, with overconfident guys appearing just as dumb as those who lack confidence altogether.

● Try to make the most of your appearance ● Try to practice speaking to someone while staring them in the eye by using a mirror ● Try to be content with who you are

Evaluate your nonverbal cues.

While all of these exercises boost your confidence, there are a few more tips I can provide that you might not have considered. How tight is your waistband? Do your feet hurt from your shoes? Are your socks smelling? Do you have fresh skin? All of these are the kinds of things that prevent you from internally feeling confident. The external world's discomforts may be quite distressing, and there's nothing more upsetting than observing a man who not only lacks confidence but also experiences physical issues like waist-aching jeans. You won't need to impose other blights on your confidence when you go out and meet people if you can learn to enjoy and take care of your physique better.

Silence and the appreciation of it both contribute to inner confidence. Take a seat by yourself and count to eight while inhaling through your nose. Let out your breath for ten counts now. Continue repeating this for around fifteen minutes, letting go of any thoughts that arise and returning to your focus each time. This helps you stay focused and composed before you go out, which enhances the visibility of your inner confidence. It's a common practice in meditation, and it's really beneficial. There are moments when your inner ideas are so abundant that they overflow and undermine your self-assurance. You'll discover that it's easier on your inner confidence and that you feel far more capable of having fun without ruining any potential meetings if you can quiet them in this manner.

Nothing is quite as appealing to a woman as a self-assured man, yet it takes a lot to win her over for a man to be secure in himself. Examine your reflection in the mirror. Appreciate how well you take care of yourself and how attractive you are. Inner confidence is more reliable than physical appearance; therefore, don't allow it to be hampered by size or lack thereof. That joyful voice inside you assures you that everything will be alright, and for the most part, it does.

Resources To Fight Your Fears

After discussing the causes of human phobias, I wanted to share with you some powerful tools for overcoming fear, which I refer to as The Prescription for Overcoming Fear. These are not exhaustive, but frequently, the success stories are really about the basics. These are easy ways to deal with your worries, face your fears, and overcome your fears.

"What you resent will persist, but what you befriend will endure," said Robin Sharma. The day you choose to face your fears head-on, learn to understand them, and remain fearful is the day you'll be able to let them go. Your worries are indicators of where you need to grow, and when you overcome them, your life will reach the highest possible levels. Here are some tools to help you overcome your worries.

1. Recognize Your Fears

Recognize which of the eight fundamental human fears most affects you. Consider these occurrences and their origins. Keep a journal, talk to someone about your concerns, or list all of your anxieties.

It's crucial to face your worries head-on and learn about them. Your hair becomes thinner when you do this. Consider them and write about them. Recognize your fears and take genuine action to solve them.

2. Confirm Your Furs

Acknowledge and experience them instead of pushing them away or acting as though they don't exist. You have to feel your worries in order to overcome them.

Avoid them at all costs; it will only take up your time. Take note of the effects they have on your body. Do you experience tightness in your chest, a knot in your stomach, or do your palms become wet? If you simply deal with the fear, it will go away. The next time you find yourself in a similar situation, and you start to feel queasy or sick to your stomach, you may say to yourself, "Oh, that's my fear of rejection; it will pass; it will pas; I recognize it, and I can deal with it." Examine the tiger in the eye.

3. Align With Your Furs

Write a letter to your friend expressing as much of your feelings as you can. Take out your diary. You don't need to show the letter to anyone, or even to yourself. Just tell your fear that your life is so much more than its confines and that you will no longer be limited by it.

If you find yourself hesitant to take a chance, consider all the negative consequences that can occur. Ask yourself if they're really so awful. Even if you failed, would you still be glad that you took a chance? You'll probably discover that failure won't lead to unpleasant consequences. You can always start over and learn from your mistakes.

4. Share Your Fears With Others

Make conversations with your friends, trusted advisors, or anybody you believe in about what you are truly afraid of, regardless of how real you believe it to be. In addition to weakening one's authority, acknowledging one's fears can lead to stronger and closer relationships with others. A different perspective from another person can help you distinguish between your unreasonable and legitimate anxieties.

Maybe she's your best friend, and you can confide in her that you're very scared of not being brave enough, of failing in relationships or falling in love. Sometimes, all it takes to get through anything is to just talk about it. It will change lives by bringing it from the subconscious to the conscious. Lift the feather and expose it to the sunlight.

5. Avoid being comfortable

Thus, a lot of people become accustomed to a certain career, relationship, or lifestyle. They avoid trying anything new since they feel comfortable in their current situation. In actuality, nothing is entirely safe. Your cosy relationship can end, and your boring but steady job could be reduced.

Avoiding risks and being comfortable in your current situation is not a reason to be afraid. Adjust so that you follow your preferences prior to being coerced by external events. Instead of settling for average or comfortable, push yourself to reach your maximum potential.

6. Confront Your Fears

Seize every opportunity to overcome your fear and elevate your life by seizing the chance. You have to do the things you are afraid of, even if you feel the dread and notice the fear. Begin with little fears and progressively increase your courage to face your biggest fears. It was once said that the fears you don't overcome become your walls. Let go of your fears, then.

Phobias are intense and persistent flutters about a specific item. Individuals suffering from phobias would do anything to avoid confronting their fears. They never confront their fear because they are escaping their phobia. Phobia treatment makes patients talk about their fears in order to help them realize that the target of their fear is not actually a threat.

Frequently, our perception of something is somewhat greater than its actuality. You will be significantly more inclined to face your concerns again if you confront them and realize that the negative effects are minimal or nonexistent.

7. Establish a Vision Board

Put it in your collage of dreams, whether you wish to travel to a faraway place, hike KĖlĖmanjaro, go on a cycle trip through Tanzania, have a baby, have a wonderful family life, or live in a big house on the hill. It provides you with a strong motivation to face your anxieties.

Be so committed to living your best life that you will just need to overcome your fears in order to get there. The ideal time to look at this collar or vĖsion bracelet is in the morning when your mind is most alert and ready for inspiration. Knowing your goals, your dreams, and what you want to create can give you the drive and tenacity to face your fears.

8. Tell a New Story to Yourself.

This recipe for conquering fear makes you reflect on your true self and your perspective. Tell a new tale, describe your life in a novel way, and express gratitude for what you have.

Oprah talks a lot about high-quality journals. I've always agreed that it's good to have a gratitude journal in which you list five things each day for which you are truly thankful. It aids in reflection and helps you move past being fearful.

9. Encircle yourself with adoration

Love is the opposite of fear. One cannot experience both fear and love at the same time. Turn life into a celebration and show gratitude. When you really give yourself over to love, you no longer worry about being rejected or not being good enough.

CHARITY AMOUNTING TO OTHERS Kindness originates from acceptance and understanding of others. Giving others the benefit of the doubt and being kind to them will greatly reduce our stress levels because we are all fallible. Attempting to transform and cure others takes away their freedom of choice while exerting control takes away our tranquillity. Being compassionate about the pain of others encourages us to act kindly toward them. Seeing someone's behaviour as an unmet emotional need that they are unable to communicate with will enable us to act with kindness. One of the most important qualities is the ability to recognize someone whose needs are not being satisfied and to act kindly toward them.

It is our task to foster compassion. How might our lives be filled with more acceptance, gratitude, compassion, and understanding? We can begin by treating ourselves to these items. Inwardly cultivating loving-kindness will be the first step on a deeply individualized path to fulfilment. The cruellest people on the planet are trapped in a mental torture chamber where they can never escape condemnation. Individuals who take the time to listen to their thoughts and reconstruct harmful messages with empathy and kindness will have begun to employ kindness's transformative potential. Our settings have the power to shape our brains through a process known as neuroplasticity. By becoming conscious of our thoughts, we may retrain our minds. Our social and emotional experiences serve as some of our most important teachers. If we don't like how we feel, we need to think and act differently. In his book on neuroscience, Richard Davidson claims that because behavioural interventions target certain brain circuits, they may be more effective than modern medical treatments. You'll experience fresh, emotional rushes as you exercise kindness both inside and outside of your body.

Kindness also helps you feel happier and more connected to other people, which lowers feelings of isolation and alienation. Acts of compassion release the hormone known as oxytocin, which promotes social connection. It has been demonstrated that when you focus on helping someone else instead of your suffering, you can overcome depression. You will feel the changes seep into you if you do this every day with a purpose connected to the welfare of others. You can develop that invigorating sensation by being good to others on a daily basis. Benefit others to benefit yourself. Humans are social creatures meant to work together for the common good. Your brain's networks will be reorganized to support emotions of fulfilment, satisfaction, and a greater purpose as you accomplish this. Even though we are taught to be self-centred, our feelings will shift if we shift our attention to how we might help others.

Self-Compassion Is Essential For Long-Term Self-Esteem

We'll look at the powerful idea of self-compassion in this chapter and see how it contributes to the development of long-lasting, robust self-esteem.

Self-Compassion: What Is It?

The capacity to show yourself the same consideration and understanding that you would show a friend is known as self-compassion. It is the discipline of showing yourself compassion, particularly while facing adversity, failing, or self-criticism.

What separates self-indulgence from self-compassion:

It is imperative to make clear that self-indulgence and self-compassion are not synonymous. It is not acceptable to neglect accountability or acknowledge mistakes when one is self-compassionate. Rather, it's about accepting your shortcomings and enduring pain with compassion, just as you would for a loved one.

The advantages of self-compassion

- Boosts Self-Esteem: Self-compassion enables you to love and accept who you are, no matter what, which boosts your self-esteem.

- Decreases Self-Criticism: You become less harsh on yourself and more likely to learn from your mistakes when you replace self-criticism with self-compassion.

Encourages Better Emotional Wellbeing: Engaging in self-compassion practices lowers stress, anxiety, and depressive symptoms, which enhances emotional well-being.

Ways to Develop Self-Compassion:

1. Self-awareness: Recognize when you are judging yourself harshly. Self-criticism can

occasionally come naturally, but you can learn to identify it.

2. Be Kind to Yourself: Show yourself kindness rather than punishing yourself. Consider how you would handle a buddy in a similar circumstance.

3. Overcome Perfectionism: Recognize that nobody is flawless. Constantly aiming for perfection might be detrimental to one's self-worth. Place a higher weight on progress instead.

4. Modify the Internal Story: Affirmations of self-compassion should take the place of negative ideas. Rather than stating, "I'm a failure," for instance, say, "I make mistakes, but that doesn't define me."

Exercise in Practice: Letter of Self-Compassion

Treat yourself to a letter written in the style of a sympathetic friend. Address your tendency toward self-criticism and extend words of encouragement and support.

Recall that practising self-compassion is a strategy for developing a positive sense of self-worth rather than a way to escape accountability. You may improve your emotional resilience and your capacity to take on obstacles head-on by learning to be kind to yourself.

In the upcoming chapter, we'll talk about the importance of good thoughts and how they affect your self-esteem.

DISCLOSING YOUR REAL SELF

You

The process of hiding one's inner self can take a lifetime, and it always starts with self-awareness. Think of the sculptor who starts a work of art with a plain marble slab. The substance itself is a fragment of the soil, honourable and lovely yet raw. It is the sculptor's job to see possibilities and bring out the best in the marble. They might envision their sculpture taking shape, and who knows? It may come to pass as vividly as it did in their minds. However, occasionally, after removing imperfections from the raw material, surprising improvements are made.

Like with a fixed perspective, there are instances when we imagine our inner selves to be one thing, but deeper reflection reveals that we are not what we imagined. We frequently find it difficult to accept who we are because we do not fully comprehend who we are. When the shape we labour to achieve does not accurately or even fairly represent our genuine form, we are left with nothing. Being authentic means letting go of self-talk that doesn't improve your connection with yourself and being honest with yourself about your true desires and inherent self. Being real is a prerequisite for growing in confidence and self-awareness. Until we let go of the façade of an imagined self, we can never be fully conscious of our innermost selves.

Ever heard of the phrase "self-fulfilling prophecy"? This phrase in sociology describes a kind of forecast that materializes only because it is taken to be true from the beginning (Schaedig, 2023). Also referred to as the law of attraction, this idea has become widely accepted because of Rhonda Byrne's best-selling book The Secret. This frequent occurrence happens when we: It's comparable to the placebo effect.

1. We tell ourselves self-made narratives about our personalities and skills.

2. By meeting specific expectations, maintain the beliefs that are ingrained in those stories.

Depending on your self-perception, allowing self-fulfilling prophecies can have both beneficial and harmful effects.

You may have told yourself a tale about how your brain isn't wired for numbers, for instance, if you conceive of yourself as someone who is so-called "right-brained" or who thinks in terms of art rather than science or math. You detest this topic at school and find it to be the worst. This belief then becomes a self-fulfilling prophesy when you decide that learning more won't do anything and don't spend enough time on it. You fail the test as a result, which confirms what you already believed. How can we possibly expect to advance or get better if we have negative self-perceptions? By establishing a connection with our true selves, we may break free from self-limiting ideas and value each other for the endless potential we each bring.

Take some time to relax and rejuvenate in nature.

Spending time in environments such as parks, gardens, farms, sanctuaries, and woods can help you feel less stressed, more at ease, and more at peace with yourself. Analyzing your ideas and ideals and making connections with them will be made easier with this, which will raise your self-esteem.

If needed, seek out professional assistance such as counselling or therapy.

Never be reluctant to seek professional counselling or therapy whenever you feel it is necessary.

Develop a growth mentality by having faith in your capacity to get better.

Never lose hope in your abilities and cognitive level; with steady effort and practice in the appropriate direction, these can be grown or improved. Having a growth mindset enables you to view obstacles as chances for development and learning. Self-esteem is enhanced when you think you can get better.

Make self-care activities a priority.

Because maintaining a healthy body and mind is necessary for having a positive sense of self.

Establish limits to safeguard your mental health.

By establishing firm limits and boundaries for interactions and forbidding others from invading your personal space or treating you disrespectfully, you can safeguard your mental well-being. Maintaining your mental health is crucial to raising your self-esteem.

You may be afraid of failing a lot, of being mistreated by people, or of a lot of other things. These anxieties keep you from acting and showing off your skills. You can only progress by challenging yourself and your abilities, so you must face your fears and step outside of your comfort zone.

Adopt the skill of saying "no" when required.

It's crucial to prioritize your demands and safeguard your time, energy, and self-worth by learning when and how to say no. By learning to say no, you can avoid overcommitting and overexerting yourself, as well as the worry that you won't be able to keep your word. It will help you feel more confident about yourself.

Appreciate the abilities of your body to cultivate a positive body image.

Instead of concentrating on your physical appearance, always remember what your body is capable of. Take up your favourite physical hobbies, such as cycling, jogging, or playing, or indulge in your artistic side with crafts or painting. Your confidence and positive self-image will increase as a result. Having confidence in your own ability boosts your self-worth.

Let go of guilt and forgive yourself for past transgressions.

You are not unique, and you may make blunders in life; after all, everyone makes mistakes. However, constantly feeling guilty and dwelling on your errors might lower your self-esteem. Instead of viewing your mistakes as a cause of self-disrespect or shame, use them as opportunities for learning and personal development and move on.

Envision yourself succeeding and realizing your goals.

Take a few minutes every day to see yourself accomplishing your objectives and leading the life of your dreams. Consider yourself to be successful. It raises self-esteem by increasing motivation and confidence.

Take part in your favourite pastimes and pursuits.

Engaging in activities related to your interests, such as singing or dancing, can lead to a feeling of contentment, joy, and relaxation. It raises your sense of self-worth and self-esteem.

To increase your sense of value, volunteer or assist others.

You will feel so worthy and wonderful about yourself when you help someone else. Along with having the ability to positively impact others' lives, you also have a sense of fulfilment in life that contributes to a higher sense of self-worth.

Use relaxation and deep breathing exercises.

Calming your thoughts and controlling tension can be achieved using deep breathing and relaxation techniques. It can lower anxiety, aid with emotion regulation, and raise self-esteem.

Recognize your self-defeating beliefs and confront them.

Determine what self-defeating thoughts you hold and write them down. These unfavourable beliefs may severely impact your self-esteem. After you've recognized them, jot down some self-affirmations and recite them aloud on a regular basis. This will improve your self-esteem and assist in getting rid of unfavourable ideas.

Make a vision board to serve as a reminder of your objectives.

Keeping a vision board helps you stay focused on your goals and life's purpose. Seeing your vision board every day helps you stay committed and boost your confidence. Making use of a vision board is beneficial when applying the law of attraction.

Put on clothing that gives you a sense of comfort and confidence.

Wearing clothes that you choose that fit you well, make you feel confident, and make you feel good about yourself helps you develop a positive self-image, which in turn helps to increase your self-esteem and confidence.

The Way We Judge Ourselves Against Others

According to the Social Comparison Theory, people gauge their value by contrasting themselves with others. In the area under comparison, those who have a good sense of self-worth would look for others who are somewhat like them and then challenge themselves to get better while setting reasonable limits.

Comparing oneself to others can lead to numerous dangers, though. It might cause sentiments of arrogance, overconfidence, or the belief that you have no right to voice complaints or raise concerns about the aim if you are continuously comparing yourself to those who are in worse situations than you. If the comparison causes you to put off achieving your objectives or have irrational expectations, it is unhealthy.

"They have half the resources and are doing more than I am, so I can't let up on my workload."

"I'll definitely win because I'm better than them."

"I manage things better than they do. I'm worthy of the advancement.

Conversely, drawing comparisons between yourself and someone you consider to be far better than you can cause feelings of resentment, jealousy, and anxiety that you will never measure up. You run the risk of setting an unachievable objective where success is determined by an arbitrary standard that is tailored to the needs of someone else.

These comparisons have the drawback of not enabling you to view the circumstances objectively. It doesn't matter about you and your unique abilities, circumstances, or efforts; rather, what matters is whether you succeed or fail based on the accomplishments of others.

We frequently use celebs in this way! Their notoriety.Their opulence.The splendour of the Kardashian way of life.The incredible athletic achievements of athletes. We believe that musicians and movie stars have it all because of their incredible charisma. That everything they could ever want is theirs, and they are prosperous and happy. However, here we are, mere mortals who will never possess the skill, good beauty, or good fortune that they were born with.

.. or were they? Do they actually have any more talent or happiness? This is how it appears from their side of the spotlight:

● Serena Williams, a tennis player and Olympic gold medallist, said to Oprah Winfrey in 2003 that she spent most of her formative years believing her sister's eating habits and overall ability to mimic her sister's behaviour determined her value. Even while it's not as awful, she admitted that she still emulates her sister in many ways.

● Nicole Scherzinger of the Pussycat Dolls disclosed that her slim and attractive appearance, which the world admired, was a result of her battle with bulimia.

● Singer and performer David Bowie concealed his struggle with feelings of inadequacy, poor self-worth, and low self-esteem behind compulsive levels of writing and performing, even in spite of the hordes of people who attended his gigs.

● After a protracted struggle with serious depression, comedian Robin Williams, who made people laugh and smile all over the world with charming and happy characters like Mrs.Doubtfire and Genie from Disney's Alladin, took his own life in 2014.

● Mariah Carey, the recipient of more than 200 music accolades, said she had always battled low self-esteem and that she felt like a "ditsy moron" to everyone.

These pillars of genius, seemingly unattainable, are similar to you and me. They have difficulty. They are concerned.

The danger of comparing yourself to others is summed up in a wonderful remark that is misattributed to Albert Einstein. "Everyone is brilliant. A fish, however, will think it is foolish for the rest of its life if you assess it by how well it can climb a tree.

How We Address Input

Those who have a healthy sense of self-worth feel at ease providing and receiving genuine compliments. They know how to accept or express gratitude for the recognition of their work without using it as a gauge of their value.

Similarly, a person with a healthy sense of self-worth can evaluate constructive criticism as an opportunity to improve and harsh criticism as something to evaluate objectively for areas that are worthwhile to focus on and things to respectfully brush off as the opinion of another person rather than a gauge of achievement and value.

Individuals who suffer from low self-esteem may minimize or deny any compliments they receive, or they may use praise from others or themselves as a barometer of their accomplishments. Negative criticism is interpreted as an assault or as "proof" of what the inner critic is saying.

How We See Failure

When they fail, people with strong self-esteem may feel wounded, but they view it as a teaching opportunity rather than a reflection of their value. It's time to take an objective look at the circumstances, reassess their objectives, and strive toward either a new or future aim.

Individuals who suffer from low self-esteem often view failure as a sign of their value or as something that they will never be able to achieve.

● They believe the test proctor is out to get them or that they are "stupid" if they fail.

● A promotion that fails indicates incompetence or an unfair advantage that someone has that they are unable to overcome.

A broken relationship indicates that the other person is naive, unattractive, or untrustworthy.

● People who quit an Ironman marathon in the first half mile are labelled as "wimps," while those who don't dedicate every waking moment to training consider the feat to be "impossible."

Failure is a barrier for someone who has a good sense of self-worth. It is an insurmountable barrier that directly affects a person's competence, value, and other facets of their self-image for people who struggle with low self-esteem.

Why Do You Have Low Self-Esteem?

What, then, accounts for your low self-esteem? Why do you think that if you make a mistake, people will laugh at you or that you are not that important? Many people lack the self-assurance necessary to handle a variety of life circumstances, and not all of them fit the stereotypical description of a "loser" as we might believe. In actuality, poor self-esteem can exist in even the most popular and successful individuals.

In all of the above instances, there is usually something wrong with your image if you are struggling with low self-esteem. Perhaps you feel like a failure and that no one would like you because you haven't had any success lately. Maybe you've been working out a lot, but you still don't look like the models you see on TV, so you think that nobody will like you. There are various reasons why your self-esteem could be low, so analyzing what is upsetting you and the source of these ideas can help you feel better about yourself.

The advantages of self-confidence are enormous. That is one of the skills that is usually needed, especially in your field of work. People with high levels of confidence are needed for a variety of job roles. Some people experience negative effects from low self-esteem, but others may feel satisfied despite having low confidence in some areas. This is acceptable, as experts and researchers argue that it's not necessary to have confidence in every facet of life.

A person's work, social relationships, and overall well-being can all be negatively impacted by disparities in these areas because low self-esteem can cause problems with communication, assertiveness, and social anxiety. People may experience feelings of worthlessness, poor ambition, a lack of purpose in life, inferiority complexes, or hatred toward other people. Making an effort to boost one's self-confidence can be quite helpful because it can help one's emotional and mental health in addition to helping one avoid obstacles in these areas. Being confident in oneself is a crucial trait that you should strive to develop.

People find confidence in self-assured individuals inspiring, and they are highly regarded. People who are self-assured face their worries head-on and are usually willing to take chances. They come to understand that they can overcome any obstacles they come across. Even when things may not be going well, self-assured people usually have a positive outlook on life and are happy with who they are.

Positively, developing self-confidence is a skill that everybody can acquire. Furthermore, it is unquestionably worthwhile to put in the effort, whether your goal is to boost your confidence or the confidence of others.

To put it simply, self-confidence is the belief in oneself and one's skills. It is an internal condition that is made up of one's feelings and thoughts about oneself. This state can change according to our current situation and how we respond to events that are going on in the world. It's quite acceptable to feel extremely confident in some circumstances and lack confidence in others.

When it comes to our confidence levels, thinking back on a past accomplishment produces a far different effect than thinking about the things we failed at.

The two main factors that affect self-confidence are self-efficacy and self-esteem.

Benefits of Self-Belief

Wellbeing and Self-Esteem: Self-confidence can be reflected in how you really feel about yourself; thus, the more self-assured you are, the more likely you are to take a risk and do something novel. There's a direct correlation between risk and success. The more success you have, the more confident and good you feel about yourself. This cycle of positivity and self-assurance repeats itself repeatedly, increasing overall happiness.

Empowerment: A person's perception of self-efficacy can be positively impacted by self-confidence. Your sense of empowerment will increase with your level of self-assurance, especially when it comes to doing new things, taking chances, and making the leap. Your level of confidence in yourself can significantly impact your ability to achieve personal goals. Because of previous achievements, difficulties frequently look less overwhelming, and you will feel strong and in charge of what is ahead.

Less Anxiety: Having self-assurance might help you feel prepared to take on obstacles. Reduced anxiety will result in less uncertainty when facing new challenges, as well as reduced worry and anxiety associated with situations that are foreign to you and frequently cause you to stumble. Instead of approaching new endeavours with reluctance, anxiety, or dread, you will approach them with optimism and learn a lot from these kinds of experiences along the way.

Less pressure, more energy: People with high levels of self-assurance may be less likely to experience anxiety and self-doubt regarding their goals and actions, which will lead to less stress. A powerful way of living that is centred on achievement and enjoyment can be encouraged by mental tranquillity.

Better Interpersonal Relationships: If happiness can be fostered by self-confidence, then relationships between individuals can also be improved as a result. Self-confident people often believe in their abilities, which makes them feel empowered and more successful than people who lack confidence. These attributes have the potential to help relationships succeed. The ability to focus attention on the needs of others as well as oneself may be enhanced by self-assurance. This independence may have an impact on a happy partnership.

Success: Every human being typically aspires to achieve success. People grow more skilled the more they accomplish. Possessing self-confidence can help you succeed by equipping you with the means to believe in your skills and to keep trying when circumstances call for perseverance and consistency.

Possessing self-confidence allows you to identify opportunities since your brain is an amazing, complex organ. A confident mind will spot possibilities, and if your goals are clear, it will start to show you all the components needed to reach them. This is due to the fact that having specific goals gives those elements context when they become apparent to you; therefore, stay vigilant at all times.

Self-confidence finds answers: When presented with a problem and you start to worry about it, your brain becomes clouded and clogged, which makes it harder to come up with an excellent solution. Being confident in yourself helps you to take a deep breath, pause, and clear your mind. It strengthens your memory, creativity, and thinking, which influences it to come up with the greatest answers to your problems.

Self-confidence boosts activity and hard work: If you lack self-confidence, it is difficult to put in the persistent effort required to attain any significant goal. Furthermore, you reinforce this lack of confidence when you fail by saying things like, "Gosh, I'm stupid!" Like, "Why the devil did I do that?" or "I'm such a loser; of course, this has happened to me!" But if you believe in yourself, you will find the will to act and sustain yourself for long periods. It will boost your self-confidence and keep you moving forward if you can accept mistakes or bad luck as part of the process and keep moving forward.

People are more receptive when you are confident in yourself. When you ask someone for anything, they will be more inclined to comply because they will sense your conviction and be more inclined to comply. Ed. In these circumstances, if your anxiety is stemming from your nerves, you should absolutely concentrate on strengthening your breathing exercises.

Freedom from self-doubt: The more self-assurance you have, the more you are able to break free from the mental torment of self-doubt and self-questioning your worth and suitability for achieving the goals you have set for yourself. We are all valued in our unique ways, and we should all be able to accomplish our goals! What makes the difference is having faith in our abilities and our commitment to working tirelessly to achieve our goals!

4. Excessive gratitude

Giving kids lots of praise for little accomplishments could seem like a smart approach to help them become more self-assured, competent, and capable actors. Many parenting experts still support this form of "positive reinforcement" today.

However, research indicates that giving youngsters unfocused praise renders it useless for them and increases the likelihood that it will lose its impact over time.

Children who receive praise for everything they do develop into "praise junkies" who are too influenced by their self-perceptions because they are accustomed to other people's opinions of them. This also raises the risk of growing up to be an adult "pleasant person" who is always looking for validation from other people. They may, therefore, frequently be "made" or "broken" by the opinions of others.

In a similar vein, our children may doubt our sincerity if we get overly enthusiastic about praising them. Put another way, if you overdo it, you can discover that your youngster eventually grows suspicious of your praise and starts to doubt its sincerity. When we behave fake around them, children become extremely sensitive. Therefore, you can start to lose children's trust and connection if you do that on a regular basis.

This particularly applies to older kids. Young children often take our words at face value, while teenagers typically have a deeper understanding of the motivations behind our words and deeds. As you age, there is some opportunity for irony and doubt, so consider this when you praise older children.

5. Use of Reward System and Sticker Chart

In recent years, rewards and sticker charts, which parents use to encourage their children to behave well and to build a good attitude toward everyday work and chores, have gained popularity.

This technique is effective in the short run, but the only thing that teaches youngsters to do politely is to get paid. In reality, studies have demonstrated that the external drive supplied by rewards is higher than the internal motivation to simply take action. In other words, if you continuously reward your child for anything today, they are essentially limiting the possibility of repeating their conduct unless more rewards spoil them.

Some parents may find it challenging to accept rewards and sticker charts because they often seem to achieve immediate and impressive outcomes. However, this compensation method does not genuinely impact their views and attitudes but rather focuses on raising children's exterior incentives. Therefore, behavioural modifications will not endure long. This is because rewards do not inspire children to think about or take responsibility for their actions, teach them "the distinction between right and wrong," and do not affect moral growth.

They are essentially a technique to bribe our children, and when rewards are eliminated, good behaviour fades with them. In the long term, parents are more likely to anticipate higher remuneration from their children. By the time they become adolescents, they may refuse to comply with your expectations without any compensation, such as monetary incentives.

6. Focus More on Your Emotions Than on Your Children's

It's only natural that we want to tell them what we're proud of. For example, parents often say, "I'm so proud of you!" and "You really moved me!"

These statements are innocent and friendly, but they are still judging children's behaviour, focusing on our thoughts on the circumstance without providing an opportunity for them to examine themselves.

Children can also perceive these remarks as indicating that it is more necessary to impress and pride parents than just participate in activities to learn, grow, and develop as human beings.

Do You Do Most of The Above? Don't Despair!

If you are used to making some or all of the mistakes listed above, don't despair. Chapter 3: Cultivating Self-Awareness

Cultivating self-awareness is a crucial step in building self-esteem. In this chapter, we will explore detailed steps to help you enhance your self-awareness and foster a strong foundation for building self-esteem.

Step 1: Reflection and Introspection

Set aside dedicated time for reflection and introspection. Find a quiet space where you can engage in deep thinking and self-exploration.

Step 2: Explore Your Values

Identify your core values—the principles and beliefs that are most important to you. Reflect on what truly matters in your life and how your actions align with your values.

Step 3: Identify Your Strengths

Reflect on your strengths and talents. Consider the activities or skills that come naturally to you and bring you joy. Acknowledge and appreciate your unique abilities and qualities.

Step 4: Uncover Your Passions

Explore your passions and interests. Pay attention to the activities that energize and inspire you. Engage in those activities regularly to foster a sense of fulfilment and purpose.

Step 5: Reflect on Past Accomplishments

Take time to reflect on your past accomplishments and successes, both big and small. Celebrate your achievements and acknowledge the effort and dedication you put into reaching those milestones.

Step 6: Embrace Growth Areas

Identify areas for growth and improvement. Be honest with yourself about the aspects of your life where you would like to see progress. Embrace a growth mindset, believing in your ability to learn and develop in those areas.

Step 7: Seek Feedback

Listen with an open mind and a willingness to learn from their insights. Use their feedback as a tool for self-improvement and personal growth.

Step 9: Regularly engage in self-reflection, exploring your thoughts and emotions on paper. Use this as a tool for self-discovery and deepening your self-awareness.

Step 10: Seek New Experiences

Embracing new experiences helps expand your self-awareness and broadens your understanding of yourself.

Step 11: Embrace Authenticity

Embrace your authentic self. Allow yourself to be true to your values, passions, and beliefs. Avoid comparing yourself to others and instead focus on being the best version of yourself.

This heightened self-awareness forms the foundation for building self-esteem, as it allows you to appreciate and embrace your unique qualities and aspirations. Stay committed to the journey of self-discovery, and watch as your self-esteem flourishes.

Self-Esteem And Self-Confidence: What Are They?

According to my research, self-esteem is the conviction that you are valuable and worthy, and it determines how you view yourself and go through life. It speaks to a person's self-assurance and competence. Being confident in oneself and one's competence is the definition of self-confidence. Self-esteem is typically built quickly in early infancy and adolescence for many people. Individuals might either have healthy or low self-esteem. A strong sense of self-worth is essential and has a significant impact on your level of success in life.

It will help to know what causes low self-esteem if you experienced difficulties with it as a teenager. Knowing the underlying reasons for low self-esteem will enable you to break free from the habits that keep most individuals stuck in the reality of having low self-esteem. Now, let's investigate the potential reasons behind poor self-esteem.

- Having an unstable attachment style as a child: When you were a young child, did your caretakers provide you space to safely express your needs? Did they meet your needs or not? Did they give you the freedom to be yourself, travel, and pursue your goals while also giving you the impression that your relationship with them will work out? If you answered "yes" to these inquiries, your positive upbringing assisted in the development of a positive sense of self. Let's say, on the other hand, that you were raised feeling as though voicing your demands would get you into trouble and that you were rejected, abandoned, afraid, and under unhealthy supervision. In that instance, low self-esteem may have naturally developed as a result of this. For someone with low self-esteem, the world seems dangerous, making it difficult to move through life with assurance and ease.

- Genetics and exposure: Have you ever observed the tendency for members of the same family to possess comparable skills or characteristics? What does your family excel at most? What is the main area of struggle for your family members? Certain families could be well-known for producing kids who excel in a specific sport or academic field. It's the same with regard to self-worth. Let's say your family is composed of strong, stable individuals and that you did not grow up in a troubled home. If so, you will likely inherit similar qualities and abilities from birth. Suppose you are exposed to self-assured individuals who have a positive sense of self from birth. In that case, you will likely begin to unconsciously and consciously take on their cognitive processes and behavioural traits as well. That's the kind of person you also become. But let's say that you come from a line of limiting ideas in your family and that you are surrounded by negativity and hopelessness all the time. If so, this will also have an impact on your confidence and help develop low self-esteem.

- Failure: Experiencing failure on a regular basis might undermine one's self-assurance and proficiency. Teens are a time when they are discovering a great deal about the world and experiencing a great deal of novelty. Teens' confidence can be severely damaged, and their self-belief weakened when they fail and then receive cruel remarks or jeers from classmates or family. In these kinds of circumstances, it might be beneficial to attempt to interpret events differently when they don't turn out as planned. Rendering a different and more positive interpretation of the circumstance will help you maintain good self-esteem instead of viewing failures as a sign of your incapacity.

You may, for example, see perceived failures as chances for personal development, exploration, adventure, and the discovery of better methods.

Signs of Poor Self-Esteem

Now, let's examine typical indicators of low self-esteem, particularly in teenagers. Certain characters may come across as arrogant if they are not thoroughly examined. However, in practice, these are typically coping strategies people use to try to mask their fears and project an air of confidence and assertiveness. It's important to keep in mind that the only thing that is liberating and incredibly magnetic is genuine confidence. The common signs of poor self-esteem are listed below.

• Making difficult choices: Acting too slowly and pursuing actions that can suggest a lack of confidence and ongoing self-doubt.

• Setting low standards for yourself: Having common goals prevents you from thinking creatively or stepping outside the norm, which leads to self-shortchanging and playing small.

• Extreme fear of doing new or difficult things: People with low self-esteem are apprehensive about trying new activities. Novelty appears frightening. It feels so much safer to stick to the pattern. This may manifest as a dread of dating someone you like, attempting new things, making new friends, or taking on challenges that the majority of your classmates find unachievable when you're a teenager.

• Finding it difficult to accept praise, encouraging words, or affection: People who have low self-esteem think less highly of themselves. This gives people the impression that they are unattractive or unattractive, insufficient and that, most of the time, whatever they do is wrong. Despite their overwhelming longing for love, they don't think they are likeable or deserving of it. Because of this, people often reject good things because they don't think they deserve them, even when they hear nice words they want to hear or when someone shows them affection.

- Dwelling on the worst-case scenarios and their flaws: Have you ever been so preoccupied with all the things you believe to be flawed about yourself? Or do you frequently find it difficult to think positively because you spend so much of your time worrying about those horrible things that might occur? This can be a sign of low self-worth.
- Inadequate, feeble, or nonexistent boundaries: Saying no is one of the hardest things for kids who are struggling with low self-esteem. They find it difficult to set boundaries for what is appropriate and to communicate their feelings. In the worst-case situation, some teenagers might not have any boundaries, giving the impression that others can treat them however they choose. Toxic behavioural

habits such as need-denying and people-pleasing are the result of this.

- Managing circumstances with a victim mentality: Having poor self-esteem frequently makes it seem as though you have no control over circumstances. You may usually react to difficulties by whining, fretting, giving up, avoiding, or fleeing. More people should have faith that they can triumph over every obstacle they face. Therefore, your mind immediately turns to thinking that you can't accomplish it, and you settle for being a victim of whatever difficulty comes your way instead of thinking of ways to win in scenarios you may find yourself in.

The chapter "How to Become an Empowered Introvert" will cover the speciality of creating meaningful connections and establishing legitimate relationships in Section 6. As a reflective individual, your ability to connect deeply with people can lead to fulfilling and long-lasting relationships. Accept your authentic self and use your reflective resources to establish meaningful relationships in personal and professional spheres.

Accepting Sincerity in Relationships

Framing authentic connections is based on legitimacy. Stay true to who you are, and let people see you for who you really are. Accept your independence and be open to sharing your thoughts, feelings, and passions. Credibility encourages communication and fosters relationships built on mutual respect and understanding.

esteeming Higher expectations without ever sacrificing

Those who are contemplative tend to favour deeper, more meaningful relationships than a large group of coworkers. Prioritize higher standards without sacrificing your relationships. Make a big investment in the people who value and respect your intellectual qualities and who positively react to your attempts to collaborate.

Complete focus and compassion

Your natural capacity for empathy and undivided attention leads to meaningful associations. Engage fully in conversations, genuinely care about the opinions of others, and offer assistance when needed. Your ability to recognize and understand a sense of intimate intimacy and trust in your relationships.

Maintaining Current Friendships Taking care of current friendships is crucial to preserving long-lasting relationships. If you're a loner, you might prefer small, one-on-one social settings to strengthen your relationships. Allocate time for sincere bonding through purposeful pursuits such as profound dialogues, mutual interests, or peaceful excursions.

Creating Room in Relationships for Isolation

While establishing connections requires work and commitment, it's essential to provide space for isolation inside them. Give your friends, family, and companions the benefit of your need for alone time by assuring them that it's not a sign of your love for them but rather a necessary aspect of your independence. Respecting and understanding each other's need for privacy leads to happy, long-lasting relationships.

Extending Empathy to Different Communication Styles

Not everyone communicates in the same way. Extend compassion and empathy to diverse communication styles, such as those exhibited by social butterflies. Recognize that some people could express their ideas more clearly and out loud, and learn to examine and appreciate these differences while staying true to your thoughtful nature.

Developing Cordial Business Partnerships

Developing positive working relationships with managers and coworkers is crucial for job success. Make the most of your capacity for undivided attention and compassion to foster a healthy work environment. Engage in team-building activities and collaborate effectively, showcasing your considerate qualities in social situations.

Accepting Our Weakness

Accepting vulnerability is often a necessary step in creating meaningful relationships. Express your thoughts and emotions honestly, even if it makes you uncomfortable at first. Weakness encourages people to form deeper bonds with you because it lets them see you for who you truly are and encourages them to do the same.

Setting Boundaries in Relationships

As you build relationships, continue setting boundaries that protect your wealth and vitality. Be specific about what you need and openly communicate your boundaries. Strong bonds take into account each other's limitations and allow room for personal growth and self-care.

Seeing Diverse Relationships

Accept the range of relationships in your daily life. As you surround yourself with individuals who have varied backgrounds and perspectives, your understanding of how the world might be understood will advance.

Developing meaningful relationships as a reflective person is a rewarding endeavour that enhances your life with meaningful and long-lasting relationships. If you embrace your introverted abilities, listen with empathy, and be genuine in your interactions, you will create relationships that offer support, joy, and a sense of belonging.

A GuideFor Developing Characteristics Of High Self-Esteem

No matter where we begin, we can all improve our sense of self-worth. Let's examine each of these ideas in more detail.

Examine Circumstances That Impact Your Self-Esteem

The people and surroundings in your immediate vicinity have a big impact on your sense of self-worth. It will be tough for you to have a good opinion of yourself if it is made up of people who make you feel inferior. However, your self-esteem will soar if encouraging and optimistic people surround you. As a result, it's critical to consider the circumstances that influence it and make an effort to alter any unfavourable ones.

Every day, make positive affirmations.

Using positive affirmations is one technique to increase your sense of self-worth. These are encouraging and upbeat things that you tell yourself. You may tell yourself things like, "I love and accept myself just the way I am," or "I am worthy of love and respect." You may raise your sense of self-worth by telling yourself these things each day.

Surrounding oneself with good individuals is a key strategy for developing strong self-esteem. These are the kind of folks who will lift you rather than bring you down. They will encourage you to pursue your objectives and aspirations and will contribute to your self-esteem. If you don't know many kind people, you should join a club or organization where you can connect with people who share your values.

Recognize your advantages and skills.

Identifying your skills and capabilities is one of the first stages toward building strong self-esteem. Everybody has different abilities; therefore, it's critical to assess what you have to give. It will give you the confidence you need to succeed and contribute in a variety of spheres of your life.

Spend some time sitting down and writing down all the things, no matter how tiny, that you are proud of having accomplished. Perhaps you always have a helping hand when someone needs it, or you listen really well. Finding your strengths, whatever they may be, is a critical first step toward building self-worth.

Apart from assessing your strengths, it's helpful to cultivate a positive self-perception. It entails embracing your imperfections and embracing who you are. Instead of concentrating on your flaws, concentrate on improving every day.

Take Your Thoughts and Make Adjustments

You should embrace your thoughts and change them for the better if you want to have a strong sense of self-worth. It implies that you must become conscious of your pessimistic beliefs and acknowledge your ability to alter them if necessary. When you find yourself having a self-defeating thought, take these actions:

• Step back and consider whether it is really the case.

• If not, discard that idea and think of something more uplifting in its stead. For instance, consider thinking, "I am working on losing weight, and I am doing great!" as opposed to, "I am so fat!"

• Recognize that your thoughts are simply that—thoughts.

Though it can appear insignificant at first, these little adjustments will have a significant impact on your self-perception over time.

Observe your physical and mental well-being.

- Maintaining good physical health requires a balanced diet, consistent exercise, and adequate sleep.
- Maintaining good mental health requires managing stress in healthy ways, such as through yoga or meditation, relaxation techniques, or counselling.
- Make sure you look good. It just means that you should take care of your hygiene and wear clothes that make you feel good about yourself, not that you have to be a model.

When you're in good physical and mental health, you'll be more equipped to face any obstacles that may arise.

ARE OUR EMOTIONS NEEDED?

Even if we no longer need to search for food and can now live in luxury homes, emotions are still essential.

The following are the top five reasons psychology specialist Kendra Cherry believes we still require our emotions:

1. To take action; 2. To endure; 3. To be safe
4. To make a decision 5. To comprehend

Mastering your emotions not only improves your understanding of others and yourself but it also facilitates understanding amongst people. People's feelings have the power to influence your own, depending on what they're saying. For instance, you immediately go on high alert and scan your surroundings for danger when you notice someone else's fearful countenance. You can't help but smile when you encounter someone who is so joyful that they can't stop smiling. Their presence makes you feel happy, too.

Our feelings serve as a warning system when something is changing in either ourselves or our immediate surroundings. Occasionally, it serves as a warning that one or both of them may be changing. Our feelings give us the knowledge we need to understand what is happening to us and how best to handle it.

Consider a scenario in which you experienced no feelings at all. How would you recognize the signs of impending danger?

Or to offer support to someone you love while they're upset? These fundamental feelings are categorized as "basic" as they are not unique to humans. These feelings are experienced by animals as well. Take, for example, the enthusiastic tail-wagging your dog does when you go home. What about the times you caught them in mischief, and they were so cutesy and guilty?

Your body and mind will be impacted by every feeling you feel. Considering how frequently our surroundings and the stimuli we are exposed to change, this is a very normal occurrence. Your body's organ in charge of generating these feelings is your brain. In particular, the limbic system.

The brain's limbic structure is divided into multiple regions. Numerous chemical messengers communicate with your limbic system.

The brain receives information from your body through these substances, which are known as neurotransmitters. Your brain will then receive these instructions and be told how it should feel. Your brain receives signals from the limbic structure when someone cuts in front of you while you're in line, telling it that you should be irritated or furious.

Realistic Steps To Teach Mindfulness:

- Meditation: Consistently practising meditation, even for short periods (10–15 minutes each day), can help develop mindfulness. Your mindfulness practice can be enhanced by a variety of meditation techniques, such as concentrating on your breathing or repeating a particular mantra.

- Mindful Breathing: Set aside some time each day to practice mindful breathing. This means focusing intently on each breath in and breath out. It offers moments of alertness and tranquillity and may be practised anywhere.

- Mindful Walking: When you stroll, especially in a natural setting, walk with awareness. Pay attention to the feel of the ground beneath your feet, the sounds in the surrounding area, and the sound of each stride.

- Body Scan: During a body scan, you should focus on every area of your body, working your way up from your toes. This can help you identify the bodily experiences that correspond with your feelings.

- Mindful Eating: Mindful eating entails being fully present during the meal, appreciating every bite, and paying attention to the flavours and textures. An important component of codependency recovery is awareness of one's relationship with food, which is fostered by this practice.

Using a Journal to Explore Yourself

It provides a disciplined way to work with your feelings, ideas, and experiences. Journaling can help uncover codependent tendencies, pinpoint triggers, and track your progress in the context of codependency treatment. Here are some advantages of journaling:

Examining Dependent Patterns Closely: By recording your interactions and relationships, you can identify patterns of codependency that come up again, such as over-indulgence in self-care, low self-esteem, or an irrational fear of being abandoned.

2. Diving into Emotions: Keeping a journal gives you the ability to explore your feelings, both in the here and now and in reaction to events in the past. This investigation makes it easier to comprehend the psychological underpinnings of codependency.

3. Clarifying thinking: Putting your ideas down on paper will aid in the clarification of your thinking, which will enable you to more easily spot erroneous or twisted views that may be the source of codependency.

4. Identification of Triggers: Keeping a journal helps identify the specific circumstances or occurrences that set off codependent reactions. You can begin to manage these triggers more skillfully if you are aware of them.

5. Monitoring Your Progress: Your notebook eventually serves as a record of your progress toward codependency recovery. Seeing the changes in your awareness and actions can be inspiring.

How to Journal Effectively: A Practical Guide:

- Set Aside a Specific Time: Make time for journaling every day or every week. For this exercise to fully benefit you, consistency is essential.

- Medium of Choice: You can use specialist journaling programs, a digital document, or pen and paper to keep a journal. Select the media that best suits your tastes.

- Uninhibited Writing: When journaling, you don't have to worry about grammar or stylistic accuracy. Without imposing self-censorship, write as honestly and freely as you can.

- Use Prompts: Consider using prompts to guide your journaling if you're not sure where to start. It might be helpful to ask questions such as "What codependent behaviours did I exhibit today?" or "What triggered my codependent response?"

- Examine and Consider: Go back over your journal entries from time to time. Think about the trends and understandings you have gained. Make use of your journal as a tool for personal development.

The journey towards self-awareness via journaling and mindfulness is ongoing. It's more important to gain a deeper understanding of oneself and the codependency that has moulded one's life than it is to achieve perfection. The following chapters of this book will explore practical methods for breaking free from codependent behaviours, setting strong boundaries, and accepting self-care and self-worth as essential elements of the healing process. Being self-aware is the cornerstone around which long-lasting change and better relationships are built.

www.ingramcontent.com/pod-product-compliance
Lightning Source LLC
Chambersburg PA
CBHW052158110526
44591CB00012B/1990